HEALTHY WEIGHT LOSS

21-DAYS MEAL PLAN

FOOD COMBINING RECIPES

Family Approved Recipes

Cooking for Two: Healthy Living Recipes, Low Fat

Roumianka Lazarova

Healthy weight loss. 21-days meal plan.

Food combining recipes

Cooking for two: healthy living recipes, low fat

Copyrights

Copyright © Roumianka Lazarova, Author, 2021

Cover and Interior design © Roumianka Lazarova, 2021

Photographs copyright© Roumianka Lazarova, 2021

All rights reserved.

Liability Disclaimer

The author reserves the right to amend, supplement, or delete parts of the book or the entire book without special notification, or to stop the publication temporarily or finally.

The author disclaims any liability for personal or commercial damages, injuries, losses, errors, omissions resulting from the use, misuse, or misinterpretation of the information provided or contrary interpretation of the subject matter herein. Despite the best-taken efforts, the author does not warrant the accuracy of the information in the book due to rapid changes of information. Any similarities with facts or people are unintentional.

This book is presented solely for informational and motivational purposes only. This book is not intended to provide medical advice of any kind or to replace medical advice, nor to diagnose, prescribe, or treat any illness, disease or injury.

ISBN: 9798521699384

Imprint: Independently published

R. Lazarova

CONTENTS

Healthy weight loss

This page intentionally left blank

INTRODUCTION

Are we eating right?

Are we eating right? We ask ourselves more often this question, but we cannot find the correct answer. How can we eliminate the bad habits that we have created over the years and prevent us from being healthy and living fully? How to choose the proper diet for us, which is not associated with painful calorie counting?

Most diets are based on the priority intake of certain substances (for example, only protein, or only fruit, etc.) and complete rejection of others. The cruel self-restrictions imposed on the necessary substances for the body always affect the body.

Today, the problem with nutrition is really quite profound. That is why more and more people are looking for the connection between our health and food choices. Proper nutrition improves the quality of life and protects us from some degenerative diseases.

I made my choice! I eat the eligible food, prepared in the right way, and I feel great. The new way of eating that I have chosen is the separate eating system, which offers a refined diet and gives me health, strength and self-confidence.

First steps in choosing a new way of nutrition

• Firstly, I looked for the mistake I make in my diet. I paid attention to what happens to our digestive system after we eat different types of food.

• The food we eat at one meal passes through the stomach in the order in which it is taken (the stomach fills up gradually, layer by layer). When we eat different foods in one meal (egg salad, soup, main course, fruit, etc.), these foods are placed in the stomach one after the other, and depending on the type of food, mixing each dish with gastric juice can take different time. If mixing is too slow, the food begins to ferment while it is still in the stomach.

• I gradually got rid of some of my bad habits. I showed the necessary self-discipline, and so the change happened calmly and without problems.

• The most challenging thing I realized I needed to change was to refuse the white sugar, the white rice, the white bread; to reduce the amount of salt; not overeating; not having dinner after a particular hour. I started eating slowly, drinking at least 8 glasses of water every day.

• I included a lot of vegetables and seasonal fruits in my daily menu. This is one of the most significant changes I have made to improve my nutrition and health.

Food combining

Food combining is not a diet but a principle of nutrition that eliminates restrictive regimes and forced correction of the body. Food combining is a dietary approach that recommends what foods (and their nutrients) can be combined and what to avoid.

The purpose of a food combining is to improve digestion and absorb nutrients more fully, taking into account the specifics of the human digestive system. It does not require forcing tastes, nor constantly overcoming natural desires by force of will, following artificially imposed rules. The basic principle is not to mix certain food groups.

It is suitable for any change in nutrition to be made smoothly, gradually without stress and tension. Getting started is easier if we remember that we should not mix protein and starchy foods. Without much care, the right combination of these foods can make us feel better - inside and out.

Applying the principle of Food Combining after the

second week, I felt that my life began to change. This easy-to-apply eating did not bother me, but the result is impressive - better health and improved vitality.

My purpose in this book is not to present the various scientific theories related to Food Combining. I adopt and apply the simplified food combination scheme. They are divided into three main groups, depending on the environment's acidity, which is necessary for their decomposition: acidic, alkaline and neutral.

The view is that acidic and alkaline foods should not enter the stomach simultaneously, but they combine freely with neutral ones. When properly combined, their maximum nutritional value is extracted with minimal strain on the digestive system.

1. Food products that require an **acidic digestive process, containing proteins**: all kinds of meat (lamb, beef, pork, beef, poultry), fish and seafood, milk and cheese, eggs, citrus fruits, etc.

Legumes (beans, peas, lentils, chickpeas) occupy a special place. Some experts believe that they are a separate group due to the relatively equal protein and starch content. To simplify things, they are referred to as products containing proteins.

2. Food products requiring an **alkaline digestive process, containing starch**: cereals (wheat, corn, rice, barley, rye, oats, millet), products thereof (flour, bread, pasta, breadcrumbs, etc.), potatoes, fruits (figs, bananas, etc.), honey, starchy vegetables.

3. Food products that require **both alkaline and acidic digestive process**. They are defined as neutral foods. These are all leafy vegetables and salads, onions, radishes, peppers, tomatoes, mushrooms, cabbage, nuts, all kinds of animal and vegetable fats, cottage cheese, and cream.

Why do diets fail?

Restrictions and deprivations are the reason for more than one or two failed diets. Large percentages of those who start a weight loss diet at some point interrupt it and return to baseline. The reason is that abstinence from certain foods is tolerated for a limited time. Prohibitions also mentally crush, so the unnatural diet does not last indefinitely.

Being overweight is a direct result of the body's difficulty coping correctly with the food we eat on a daily basis. The body does everything possible to keep its reserves. It is built in such a way that in times of restrictions, it uses its stocks infinitely economically and even tries to accumulate new ones. Therefore, the regulation of weight by the amount and type of food we serve to the body is not strong enough. It works for a short time.

Weight Loss with Food Combining Recipes

The food combining is one of the alternative ways for healthy, lasting and problem-free weight loss. The food combining does not deny types of food but reforms the way they are combined. The limitations are in the combination. It is a principle in which we really eat everything, and again we model our weight, which corresponds to the structure and natural features of each person's body. The body does not feel the lack and is not provoked to accumulate reserves.

Food combining diet is actually too easy!

I know from personal experience that rapid weight loss is not healthy. Any change in nutrition should be gradual. It is common to think that we gain weight because we eat large amounts of food. In many cases, weight gain is more an expression of nutritional imbalance than overeating.

Since I embarked on the path of food combining eating, I have never felt psychological discomfort. My metabolism has been normalized.

I developed a habit of separating incompatible foods, and my weight began to decrease without much effort.

Here are some very simple tips that helped me lose weight and reach the desired weight:

1. Positive thought and belief that what I do is important to me, I like it, and it brings me actual results.

2. I eat moderately (less than before). I do not eat out of habit if I am not hungry! I only eat when I am hungry. I forgot about midnight meals, eating in front of the TV or while working.

3. My breakfast is light and possibly alkaline: fruit, yoghurt with fruit or freshly squeezed orange juice or other fruit. I am not afraid of a lack of energy for the coming day.

4. I prepare lunch and dinner according to the recipes in this book. The dishes are delicious, the portions modest. I often include vegetable salads, which contribute to a more complete diet.

5. I use fat and cheese sparingly. I prefer unsalted cottage cheese or fresh mozzarella cheese. I do not include butter sauces in my daily menu. I season salads with a limited amount of vegetable fat.

6. I take fruits as a separate dish. They do not combine well with bread, cereals, pasta, meat, and fish. The fruits, taken on their own, are easily and quickly processed. It is good to be taken slowly, in moderate amounts. Fresh fruit juice is equivalent to fruit, making digestion even more accessible.

7. I imperceptibly reduced the amount of food because the portions in the recipes in this book are successfully and precisely selected.

8. I drastically reduced the amount of salt.

9. I avoid certain foods - bread, carbohydrates, saltines, biscuits, chips, pastries, soft drinks, candy, ice cream or other foods that contain sugar or artificial sweeteners.

10. I do not sweeten coffee and tea.

11. Drink enough water (7 - 8 glasses). Here I do not include the amount of juice, coffee or tea.

12. I refrain from eating between main meals. If I cannot stand it, I eat some raw sunflower seeds.

How the menu is composed in this book

At food combining, everyone can use their imagination for new recipes and delicious dishes and adapt them to their new eating habits.

This book offers menus for 21 days. The basic principle of food combining is observed: proteins and starchy recipes are included in separate meals - lunch or dinner. It is best to leave enough time between these meals for the stomach to digest the food and empty.

When compiling recipes and combining them for each day (lunch and dinner), small amounts of adequately combined foods are included, which are easily digested. It is not essential to eat a large amount of food, but it should be easily digested, processed and assimilated by our body.

The idea of this 21-day diet is to clearly separate foods containing protein and starch. The combining is simple and clear, without compiling tables, prohibitory lists of products or the number of calories for each serving.

It is sufficient to imagine that the day we **have a protein lunch - the dinner is starchy**. For the next day, we plan **a starchy lunch - protein dinner**, and so we alternate according to this scheme for 21 days. Breakfast is usually alkaline. **Alkaline, starchy and protein eatings are included every day, so our body receives all kinds of substances.**

For protein meals are included: lean meats - chicken, turkey, beef, fish and seafood, eggs and fresh cheese. Two, three or more different types of protein are not mixed in one recipe (or menu). For example, if lunch is fish, it is not combined with cheese, chicken, eggs or meat.

Vegetable proteins are obtained from legumes (lentils, beans, chickpeas).

Protein recipes *for lunch or dinner* are appropriately combined with neutral products (vegetables, mushrooms, sauces).

Starchy recipes for lunch or dinner also contain compatible products selected to be compatible with the salads or sauces offered to them.

Products to implement the recipes in this book

It is essential to plan your daily menu. These 21-day food combining meal plan recipes will help you do just that.

The meat (chicken, turkey, pork, beef), fish and seafood must be fresh. Only in exceptional cases can a fresh-frozen product be allowed.

Free-range eggs.

Fresh vegetables and fruits. It is best to buy on the day of use. Do not overstock, do not store them in a fridge. Set aside a special cool place for them.

Brown rice is used for starchy dishes. Compared to white rice, it contains 300% more **vitamin B**.

The fats used are: Extra Virgin Olive Oil, cold-pressed sunflower oil, butter (unsalted or slightly salted).

The use of **salt** as a spice in recipes is written as "salt to taste". This is my message about the very limited use of salt. The sea salt contains valuable trace elements, and that is why I prefer it.

To enhance the taste, it is good to use **fresh and dried herbs** (parsley, coriander, dill, basil, rosemary, thyme, etc.) and spices. They reduce the need for salt.

Apple cider vinegar is preferred for flavouring salads.

Buckwheat and quinoa are increasingly used in modern cuisine.

Oatmeal is excellent for breakfast or porridge.

Nuts are a highly concentrated food. They contain fats and proteins. They are unadulterated food with which you can replace protein. The most valuable are the almonds, which practically do not contain starch, but 25% protein, 50 -55% fat.

Use dishes with non-stick bottom: pans and pots;

Cooking methods are **sautéing, cooking and baking in the oven or on the grill.** Frying is not allowed.

This page intentionally left blank

BREAKFAST RECIPES

I left the rich, greasy and heavy snacks in my past. Now that I have chosen a healthy lifestyle, I start my day with a light, wholesome, vitamin breakfast. In a separate diet, the best choice is one of two types: alkaline breakfast or starchy breakfast.

ALKALINE BREAKFAST

If we want to speed up our weight loss, it is good to start the day with an alkaline breakfast. Most often, these are fruit-milk mixtures. They include sour fruits (fresh or dried), yoghurt and, optionally, some raw sunflower or pumpkin seeds, ground almonds or hazelnuts.

Fruits suitable for alkaline breakfast: apples, peaches, nectarines, apricots, bananas, mangoes, papayas, oranges, grapefruit, kiwi, lemon, cherries, strawberries, raspberries, dates, figs.

For my alkaline breakfast, I use the following combinations:

• 1 cup of yoghurt and added ½ a cup of fruit (strawberries, cherries, or grated apples, peaches, apricots or cut into small pieces figs, oranges, etc.)

• Juice of 1 grapefruit or orange

• Yogurt with grated fruit (I choose fresh ripe seasonal fruits) and one teaspoon of sunflower or raw pumpkin seeds

• Yogurt with two finely chopped dried apricots and 1 tablespoon of wheat germ

• Mixture of 3 tablespoons yoghurt, 1 grated small sour apple, 1-tablespoon oatmeal, 1-tablespoon lemon juice, 1-tablespoon ground raw almonds. Serve immediately.

STARCH BREAKFAST

• 2 thin slices of wholemeal bread spread with butter

• 2 thin slices of wholemeal bread with 1 slightly ripe avocado and lemon juice

• 1 cup oatmeal with dates, flaxseed and ½ tablespoon ground almonds

• 4 tablespoons raw oatmeal, a pinch of cinnamon, ½ tablespoon ground almonds pour hot water, stay overnight, then add ½ banana and serve

• 3 tablespoons boiled quinoa, a pinch of cinnamon, ½ a tablespoon of ground almonds and a few raisins

• 3 tablespoons boiled buckwheat with ½ tablespoon ground hazelnuts and 2 dried figs, finely chopped

LUNCH AND DINNER RECIPES

DAY 1

LUNCH: Baked Almonds Crusted Fish

Parsley Salad with Olives

Servings: 2

Ingredients:

- 14 oz (400 g), 2 Loch trout fillets (or salmon)
- 3 tablespoons crushed almonds
- 1 teaspoon sesame tahini
- 1 tablespoon fresh lemon juice
- 2 teaspoon olive oil

Spices: a pinch of sea salt, a pinch of ground black pepper.

Instructions:

Preheat the oven to 410 F / 210 C. Grease a baking tray with oil.

Combine 2 tablespoons of crushed almonds, tahini, and 1-teaspoon olive oil in a small bowl. Stir until evenly combined.

Rub trout fillets with lemon juice. Lightly season with salt and pepper on both sides.

Grease with almonds mixture, pressing the mixture down onto fillets.

Bake in the preheated oven for 6 minutes. Place the hot fish into 2 individual serving plates. Sprinkle the fish fillets with the remaining crushed almonds.

Serve with: Parsley Salad with Olives.

Ingredients: 4 tablespoons finely chopped parsley; 7 oz (200 g) cherry vine tomatoes, halved; 1 spring onions, finely chopped; 10 pitted black olives; 1 tablespoon fresh lemon juice; 4 lemon wedges.

Instructions: Prepare the salad just right before serving. Put all the ingredients in a bowl. Stir gently until thoroughly mixed. Garnish with lemon wedges.

DINNER: Spicy Cauliflower Rice

Garnish: Garlic Sauce

Servings: 2

Ingredients:

- 14 oz (400 g), cauliflower
- 1/3 red bell pepper, finely chopped
- 1 small onion, finely chopped
- 1 teaspoon ginger, grated
- 1 clove garlic, grated
- 2 tablespoons olive oil or sunflower oil

Spices: 1-teaspoon ground turmeric, 1-teaspoon ground cumin, ½-teaspoon ground coriander, ½-teaspoon garam masala, a pinch of ground black pepper, salt to taste.

Instructions:

Rinse the cauliflower, cut into florets and dry with a kitchen towel. Place cauliflower in a food processor or blender and pulse until finely chopped (rice).

Heat olive oil in a frying pan over medium heat. Add the onions, ginger, red bell pepper and garlic, stir for 2 minutes. Then add all spices, stirring continuously for ½ minute. Add the cauliflower rice and cook for 3 minutes, stirring.

Serve with: Garlic Sauce

Ingredients: 1-cup Greek-style natural yogurt, 2 grated cloves garlic, 1-tablespoon lemon juice, a teaspoon grated lemon peel.

Instructions: In a bowl, combine all ingredients. Serve 2 tablespoons of sauce to each portion.

DAY 2

LUNCH: Buckwheat Spinach

Cucumber Mint Salad

Servings: 2

Ingredients:

- 7 oz (200 g) fresh baby leaf spinach, washed and ready to eat
- 1/3 cup buckwheat
- 2 spring onions, chopped
- 1 teaspoon ginger, grated
- 1 carrot, finely chopped
- 1 ½ cup hot water
- 3 tablespoons olive oil

Spices: a pinch of chilli powder, 1-tablespoon fresh garden mint, 1 tablespoon finely chopped parsley, 1 tablespoon finely chopped fresh dill, ground black pepper to taste, and sea salt to taste.

Instructions:

Rinse the buckwheat with cold water.

Heat oil in a saucepan over medium-high heat. Add and

saute onion, ginger, and carrot for 2 minutes, stirring occasionally. Then add a pinch of chilli powder and hot water. Bring to a boil. Add the buckwheat, put the lid, reduce heat to low and simmer for 3 minutes. Add the spinach, sea salt, black pepper, stir and cook for 3 minutes on low heat. Remove from heat. Add the garden mint, parsley and dill, stir and cover. Serve after 15 minutes.

Serve with: Cucumber Mint Salad.

Ingredients: 1 whole cucumber, 2 spring onions, 2 teaspoons olive oil, apple cider vinegar to taste, fresh mint to taste, salt to taste.

Instructions: Rinse the cucumber with cold water. Cut into thin disks. Arrange them on a wide serving plate. Sprinkle cucumbers with finely chopped onions. Garnish with garden mint. Before serving, season with salt, olive oil and vinegar.

DINNER: Grilled Bacon Wrapped Chicken Breast

Roasted Peppers Tricolour Salad

Servings: 2

Ingredients:

- 2 fresh boneless, skinless chicken breast, halves

- 4 streaky smoked bacon
- Spices: 2 small sprigs of fresh rosemary, ground black pepper to taste

Instructions:

Place chicken breast between two pieces of plastic wrap on a cutting board and thin with a meat tenderizer or rolling pin.

Season the chicken breast on all sides with black pepper. Lay one rosemary sprig on the chicken breast.

Wrap each chicken breast in 2 streaky smoked bacon to hold the rosemary on, overlapping each slice to secure. To secure the bacon not to become unwrapped on the grill, you can also use toothpicks.

Heat grill to medium-high heat. Add a small amount of vegetable oil on a folded piece of paper towel, and then carefully grease the grill with the oil. (Can use Non- flammable cooking spray to grease grill)

Place the chicken breast on the grill. Cook until no longer pink in the centre and the juices run clear,   6 minutes on per side. Remove the toothpicks before serving. Allow the chicken to rest uncovered for 5 minutes and serve.

<u>Serve with:</u> Roasted Peppers Tricolour Salad

Ingredients: 1 medium size red bell pepper, 1 medium orange bell pepper, 1 medium yellow bell pepper, 2 tablespoons pitted black olives, 1 spring onions, 1 tablespoon olive oil, 2 teaspoons apple cider vinegar, 2 tablespoons finely chopped parsley, a pinch of sea salt

Instructions: Place the peppers to grill, occasionally turning, until on all sides tender, about 10 minutes. Transfer to a bowl, cover tightly with plastic wrap and set aside 20 minutes. Remove skin and seeds. Cut each pepper lengthwise into 8 pieces. Arrange roasted peppers on a serving platter, drizzle with olive oil and vinegar. Season with salt, add olives and sprinkle with finely chopped spring onions and parsley.

DAY 3

LUNCH: Roasted Pork & Beef Meatballs

Fresh Arugula Salad

Serving: 2

Ingredients:

- 3.5 oz (100 g) beef mince, 5% fat
- 7 oz (200 g) pork mince, 5% fat
- 1 leek (only the white part), finely chopped
- ½ cup fresh mushrooms, finely chopped
- 3 tablespoons sunflower oil

Spices: 1-teaspoon fresh thyme, 2 tablespoons finely chopped parsley, ground black pepper to taste, a pinch of sea salt.

Instructions:

Preheat the oven to 390 F / 200C.

Heat 2 tablespoons oil in a saucepan over medium-high heat and saute mushrooms and leeks for 3 minutes. In a large bowl, combine beef mince, pork mince, mushrooms and leeks. Add all spices and mix well. Shape mixture into balls (the number depends on their size). Grease a baking tray with oil.

Place the meatballs, grease with the remaining oil. Bake in the oven for 30 minutes or until golden brown.

Serve with: Fresh Arugula Salad.

Ingredients: a handful of arugula, ½ Iceberg lettuce, 2 radishes, and 2 finely chopped spring onions, a pinch of salt, 2 teaspoons olive oil

Instructions: Wash vegetables before use. Put in a large bowl, season with salt and oil. Serve immediately with meatballs.

DINNER: Garlic Green Beans

Garnish: Sour Cream Sauce

Servings: 2

Ingredients:

- 1 lb (450 g) green beans (fresh or frozen)
- 5 whole cloves garlic
- 1 yellow onion, diced
- 1 medium carrot, diced
- 3 tablespoons vegetable oil
- 1 teaspoon tomato paste

Spices: salt to taste, 1 teaspoon sweet paprika, 1

tablespoon finely chopped parsley, 1 tablespoon finely chopped dill

Instructions:

Clean the green beans and wash them thoroughly with cold water.

Heat the oil in a saucepan over medium-high heat. Add and saute onion and carrot for 2 minutes. Add the garlic, chilli pepper and tomato paste. Stir, add the sweet paprika and green beans. Pour with 1.5 cups of warm water, and season with salt and cook on low heat. When the liquid evaporates, remove the saucepan from the heat. Stir in parsley and serve in individual plates with garnish.

Serve with: Garnish Sour Cream.

Ingredients: 4 tablespoons sour cream, 1 tablespoon lemon juice, a pinch of sea salt, a pinch of ground black pepper, 1 baby grated cucumber, ½ tablespoon finely chopped dill

Instructions: In a small bowl, mix sour cream, lemon juice, dill, cucumber, dill, salt and black pepper. Add 2 tablespoons of the garnish to each serving.

DAY 4

LUNCH: Summer Vegetable Stew

Cabbage Salad

Servings: 2

Ingredients:

- 1 medium zucchini, diced
- ½ small eggplant, diced
- ½ bell peppers (yellow or orange or red), thinly sliced
- 1green chillies, finely chopped
- 1 yellow onion, thinly sliced
- 2 clove garlic, minced
- 5 Roma tomatoes, diced
- 2 tablespoons olive oil

Spices: 1-teaspoon sweet paprika, salt to taste, seasoning mixture (marjoram, fennel, basil).

Instructions:

Heat the olive oil in a large frying pan over medium-low heat. Add the onions and garlic, saute for 2 minutes, stirring occasionally. Add the eggplants and saute for 5 minutes or until they have softened. Stir in the zucchini, bell peppers, green chillies, paprika, and salt. Cook over medium heat, occasionally stirring, for 5 minutes and add tomatoes. Cover and sauté 8 minutes. Stir in seasoning mixture. Remove from heat.

Serve with: Cabbage Salad.

Ingredients: 2 cups sweetheart cabbage, 2 tablespoons sunflower oil, salt to taste, 2 tablespoons finely chopped fresh leaf parsley, apple cider vinegar to taste (optional).

Instructions: Rinse sweetheart cabbage and dry with paper towels. Cut into thin strips. Put in a bowl the cabbage, parsley, salt, oil, apple cider vinegar to taste and mix just right before serving.

DINNER: Turkey Steak with Mushroom Sauce

Fresh Mix Leaf Salad

Servings: 2

Ingredients

- 2 fresh turkey breast steaks
- 1 yellow onion, chopped
- 6 oz (170 g) fresh sliced mushrooms portabella
- 1 teaspoon butter
- 2 tablespoons sunflower oil

- 1 cup chicken broth

Spices: 1fresh teaspoon thyme, oregano to taste, ground black pepper to taste, salt to taste, 2 tablespoons finely chopped parsley, crushed red pepper (flakes) to taste.

Instructions:

Rub steaks with salt and black pepper. Heat butter and oil in a large non-stick skillet over medium-high heat. Place steaks on the skillet, cook for 3 - 4 minutes on each side. Remove from heat.

In the same skillet, put thyme, oregano and mushrooms to braise for 2 minutes (without stirring). Then stir and add onion, cook 2 minutes. Remove it and add it to the steaks. In the skillet, pour chicken broth, constantly stirring. Bring to a boil. Return the steaks and mushrooms. Season with salt and pepper. Cover up; simmer over low heat for 30 minutes.

Remove from heat, season with crushed red pepper (optional) and parsley.

Serve with: Fresh Mix Leaf Salad.

Ingredients: 5 oz (140 g) fresh spring mix leaf salad, 2 chopped, spring onions, and dressing (1-tablespoon olive oil, 2 tablespoons lemon juice, a pinch of salt)

Instructions: Put leaf salad and onions in a bowl. Pour the dressing and mix just right before serving.

DAY 5

LUNCH: Mediterranean King Prawns

Servings: 2

Ingredients:

- 10.5 oz (300 g) cooked and peeled large king prawns
- ½ yellow onion, chopped
- 2 cloves garlic, finely chopped
- ½ red bell pepper, finely chopped
- 12 oz (340 g) fresh tomatoes or (canned tomatoes, diced)
- 2 tablespoons capers (washed thoroughly with water)
- 2 tablespoons pitted green olives, sliced
- 1/3 cup hot water
- 1 tablespoon olive oil

Spices: 2 tablespoons lemon juice, a small sprig of fresh rosemary or a pinch of dried rosemary, 2 stems of fresh thyme or ½ teaspoon of dried thyme, ground black pepper to taste, sea salt to taste, 6 torn leaf fresh basil.

Instructions:

First, put the raw prawns in a deep bowl. Add lemon

juice, a tablespoon olive oil, and stir. Let stand 15 minutes.

Heat the oil in a non - stick skillet over medium heat, and saute onion, garlic, red bell pepper, rosemary, thyme for 4 minutes, stirring occasionally. Then add the tomatoes, hot water, olives and capers. When the mixture thickens, add the prawns. Season with black pepper and salt; simmer on low heat for 2 minutes. Remove from the heat. Sprinkle with basil and serve.

DINNER: Tricolour Rotini Pasta

Servings: 2

Ingredients:

- 8 oz (225 g) Italian tri-colour Rotini Pasta
- 1-teaspoon sea salt

For the sauce: 2 teaspoons olive oil, 1 – 2 clove garlic, ¼ finely chopped fennel, 1 medium carrot, 1 cup tomatoes - diced, a pinch of ground black pepper, a pinch of sea salt.

Instructions:

Pour 8 cups of water into a large pot. Bring to a boil. Add 1-tablespoon salt and pasta. Cook for about 9 minutes, stirring occasionally.

Meanwhile, prepare the sauce. Finely chop the garlic, carrot and fennel. Heat olive oil in a saucepan over medium heat. Add the vegetables and saute for 2 minutes, occasionally stirring. Then add tomatoes, salt and pepper, cook for 2 -3 minutes. Remove from heat.

Drain pasta, stir in sauce and serve.

DAY 6

LUNCH: Creamy Coconut and Broccoli Soup

Garnish: Croutons with Oregano

Servings: 2

Ingredients:

- 1 ½ cups of broccoli florets
- 1 small onion, chopped
- 1 medium carrot, chopped
- ½ cup celery, chopped
- ½ cup potato, chopped
- 1 teaspoon grated ginger
- 1-cup coconut milk
- 1-teaspoon butter and 1-tablespoon olive oil

Spices: 2 stems of fresh thyme, a small sprig of fresh rosemary, a pinch of ground nutmeg, 1 teaspoon ground cumin, salt to taste, ground black pepper to taste, juice of ½ lemon.

Instructions:

In a saucepan, pour 3 cups of hot water, cumin, nutmeg, salt, black pepper and broccoli florets. Bring to a boil. Cook over low heat, about 3 minutes. Remove the saucepan from the heat. Drain the broccoli. Set aside. Discard the water.

Heat the butter and oil in a large saucepan over medium-high heat. Add the onion, ginger, carrot, celery, potato, thyme, and rosemary; saute for 2 - 3 minutes, stirring occasionally.

Pour 2½ cups of hot water, a pinch of salt and black pepper. Bring to a boil. Cook over low heat, about 20 minutes. Remove from the heat.

Working in batches, puree the mixture in a blender until very smooth. Transfer the soup to another saucepan. Stir in the coconut milk and bring to simmer over low heat for 2 - 3 minutes, stirring. Then add broccoli florets, and after 1 minute, remove the soup from the heat and ladle it into bowls. Add a juice of lemon at will.

Serve with: Croutons with Oregano.

Ingredients: 2 – 3 medium slices wholemeal bread, 1 – 2 teaspoons olive oil, a pinch of oregano, a pinch of ground black pepper

Instructions: Preheat the oven to 390 F / 200C. Cut bread into small cubes. Put the bread in a baking tray. Season with oregano, ground black pepper and olive oil, stir and bake until browned. Remove from the oven. Let cool.

DINNER: Grill Pork Fillet Medallions

Garnish: Rainbow Chard

Servings: 2

Ingredients:

- 4 pork fillet medallions

Spices: 2 tablespoons sunflower oil, ground black pepper to taste, salt to taste.

Instructions:

Preheat the grill for medium heat. Add a small amount of vegetable oil on a folded piece of paper towel, and then carefully grease the grill with the oil.

Rub the medallions on both sides with sunflower oil. Season with salt and ground black pepper.

Place the medallions on the grill or grill pan. Cook for 4 minutes on each side (or until juices run clear and no pink colour remains). Remove the medallions from the grill. Place under aluminium foil to rest for 5 minutes before serving.

<u>**Serve with:**</u> Rainbow Chard with Sunflower Seeds.

Ingredients: 2 stalks colour rainbow chard or about 2 cups greens and sliced stems, ½ small white onion finely chopped, 1 small Granny Smith apple cut into fine sticks, 1 tablespoon olive oil, 2 tablespoons lime juice, salt to taste, ground black pepper to taste, 2 tablespoons sunflower seeds

Instructions: Rinse chard with cold water, dry with a kitchen towel and trim its ends. Slice the stems in thin slices (about 1/8 inch, 0.3 cm). Put them in a large bowl. Slice the large leaves lengthwise into small tender pieces. Add to the bowl with stems, along with the onion. Cut the apple into very thin slices; pour with 1-tablespoon lime juice. Add the apples, season with olive oil, 1-tablespoon lime juice, salt and ground black pepper to taste; mix gently. Finally, add the sunflower seeds to the top of the chard.

DAY 7

LUNCH: Eggplant Boats with Turkey

Romaine lettuce Cucumber Salad

Servings: 2

Ingredients:

- 2 medium eggplants
- 11 oz (310 g) fresh turkey mince, 2% fat
- 1 onion, finely chopped
- 2 cloves garlic, grated
- 11 oz (310 g) fresh tomato, cut into thin disks
- 4 tablespoons olive oil
- ½ cup vegetable stock

Spices: ½-tablespoon Worcestershire sauce, 2 stems of fresh thyme, 3 tablespoons finely chopped fresh parsley, 1 teaspoon sweet paprika, sea salt to taste, ground black pepper to taste.

Instructions:

Preheat the oven to 390 F / 200 C. Line a baking dish with foil.

Cut eggplants in half lengthwise. Carefully carve the inside. Chop and reserve about ¼ for the stuffing.

Heat 2 tablespoons olive oil in a large pan over medium-high heat. Add onion, garlic, thyme, reserved chopped eggplants, salt and pepper and saute for 3-4 minutes. Then add turkey mince, cook and stir until broken into tiny pieces, 5 – 7 minutes. Add sweet paprika, Worcestershire sauce and vegetable stock. Simmer until mixture reduces, about 10 – 12 minutes. Remove from heat, add parsley and stir.

Place eggplants boats in the foil-lined dish and stuff evenly with the turkey mixture. Arrange the tomatoes on top. Pour 2 tablespoons olive oil and bake in the preheated oven for about 30 – 40 minutes.

Serve with: Romaine Lettuce Cucumber Salad.

Ingredients: Romaine lettuce leaves, half cucumber - cut into half-moons, ¼ red onions – sliced thinly, 6 green olives. **Dressing:** 2 teaspoons olive oil, apple cider vinegar to taste, salt to taste.

Instructions: Wash romaine leaves well and dry. Cut crosswise into 0.5-inch (1.2 cm)-wide pieces. Whisk olive oil, apple cider vinegar and salt in a small bowl. Put in a bowl the lettuce leaves, cucumber, onions and olives. Pour the dressing and mix just right before serving.

DINNER: Baked Hasselback Potatoes

Beetroot and Iceberg Salad

Servings: 2

Ingredients:

- 2 large baking potatoes
- 4 tablespoons sour cream
- 4 teaspoons melted butter

Spices: sea salt to taste, ground black pepper to taste, fresh oregano (or dried) to taste and sweet paprika.

Instructions:

Wash the potatoes with cold water and dry with paper towels.

Place each potato between two cutting boards. Then, with a sharp knife, make vertical slits in the potato 0.4 inch (1 cm) apart, being sure to stop at least before the bottom (do not cut all the way through).

Line a baking tray with aluminium foil; coat it with cooking sunflower oil spray. Place the potatoes on the baking tray.

Brush the melted butter over the potatoes, making sure to get some in between the slices, sprinkle salt and black pepper.

Preheat the oven to 400 F / 205 C.

Roast the potatoes until tender, golden brown, and crisp for 45 minutes. Then remove the potatoes from the oven. Put sour cream and sweet paprika in between each cut of the potatoes. Return the baking tray to the oven and roast for 5 minutes.

Serve immediately. Sprinkle each potato with oregano (optional).

Serve with: Beetroot and Iceberg Salad.

Ingredients: ½ Iceberg lettuce - torn into 0.5-inch (1.2 cm)-wide pieces, ½ cup beetroot - peeled and diced, 2 spring onions - finely chopped, 2 tablespoons pomegranate grains, 1tablespoon olive oil, lemon juice to taste, 2 tablespoons finely chopped fresh parsley, a pinch of sea salt

Instructions: Put all ingredients in a large bowl and mix just right before serving.

DAY 8

LUNCH: Fish and Mussels Soup

Servings: 2

Ingredients:

- 9 oz (255 g) white fish fillets, cut into small pieces
- 10 mussels
- ½ yellow onion, finely chopped
- 2 celery sticks, finely chopped
- 1 cup tomatoes, diced
- 2 cloves garlic, grated
- 1 tablespoon olive oil
- 2 cups vegetable stock

Spices: 2 stems of fresh thyme, 1 tablespoon fresh leaves coriander, salt to taste, ground black pepper to taste, 4 lemon wedges.

Instructions:

Do not put open mussels! Discard them!

Heat olive oil in a soup pot over medium heat. Add onion, celery, garlic, thyme, salt, pepper and saute for 2 - 3 minutes. Then add the fish, mussels, tomatoes and stir. Pour vegetable stock, bring to a boil. Simmer about 10 – 12 minutes.

Remove from heat, add coriander and stir. Serve in individual bowls with lemon wedges.

Note: *If there are mussels that have not opened - discard them.*

DINNER: Mushrooms Quinoa

Colourful Vegetable Salad

Servings: 2

Ingredients:

- 1/3 cup quinoa
- 2/3 cup vegetable stock
- ¼ red bell peppers, thinly sliced
- 3.5 oz (100 g) mushrooms, sliced
- 1 /4 white onion, finely chopped
- 1 clove garlic, grated
- 1-teaspoon butter

Spices: 2 stems of fresh thyme, ½ teaspoon fresh rosemary, 2 tablespoons finely chopped parsley, salt to taste, ground black pepper to taste, 2 lemon wedges

Instructions:

Pour the quinoa with 2 cups of cold water. Let for 2-3 hours. Then rinse thoroughly with cold water. In a saucepan of 2/3 cup vegetable stock, cook quinoa for 10 minutes, remove from heat. Set aside.

Heat butter in a skillet over medium-high heat. Add onion, mushrooms, red bell peppers, garlic, thyme, rosemary, and saute for 3 minutes, stirring occasionally. Season with salt and pepper to taste. Stir in quinoa until well combined. Serve immediately in individual plates. Garnished with parsley and lemon wedges.

Serve with: Colorful Vegetable Salad.

Ingredients: 1 handful arugula, 4 cherry tomatoes – halves, half cucumber – cut into half-moons, 1 handful fresh baby leaf spinach - washed and ready to eat, 2 spring onions - finely chopped, 1 tablespoon olive oil, lemon juice to taste, 2 tablespoons finely chopped fresh parsley, a pinch of sea salt

Instructions: Put all ingredients in a large bowl, and mix just right before serving.

DAY 9

LUNCH: Whole-wheat Spaghetti

Tomato Almonds Sauce

Servings: 2

Ingredients:

- 8 oz (225 g) whole-wheat spaghetti
- 1-teaspoon sea salt

For the sauce: 2 teaspoons olive oil, 1 cup tomatoes - diced, 1 oz (28 g) crushed almonds, ½ handful torn fresh basil leaves, a pinch of ground black pepper, a pinch of sea salt

Instructions:

For the sauce: Heat olive oil in a saucepan over medium heat. Add the tomatoes and saute for 2 minutes, occasionally stirring. Then add crushed almonds, ground black pepper, salt and basil, stir and remove from heat.

Pour 6 cups of water into a large pot. Bring to a boil. Add 1-teaspoon salt and pasta. Cook for about 9 minutes, stirring occasionally. Drain pasta, stir in sauce and serve.

DINNER: Traditional Osso Buco

Garnish: Gremolata

Servings: 2

Ingredients:

- 1 lb (450 g) veal shank (or lamb)
- ½ yellow onion, chopped
- 2 cloves garlic, finely chopped
- 1 medium carrot, chopped
- 1 cup tomatoes, diced
- 1 teaspoons butter
- 1 cup veal stock or hot water

Spices: 2 stems of fresh thyme, salt to taste, ground black pepper to taste

Instructions:

Season veal shank with salt and pepper. Melt the butter in a non – stick frying pan over medium heat. Add veal shank, and cook on each side for 2 minutes or until browned on the outside. Remove from heat, set aside. In the same pan, add the onion, garlic, carrot and thyme; saute for 2 – 3 minutes, stirring occasionally. Return the veal shank to the pan; add tomatoes, veal stock (hot water), a pinch of salt and pepper. Cover, and reduce heat to low and simmer for 90 minutes. Turn the meat every 15 minutes (use tongs). The meat should be tender (not falling off the bone). Serve the dish on individual plates. Garnished with gremolata.

Serve with: Gremolata

Ingredients: 3 tablespoons finely chopped parsley, 1 minced clove garlic, 1 tablespoon lemon zest

Instructions: In a small bowl, mix all ingredients. Sprinkle the gremolata and serve.

DAY 10

LUNCH: Vegetable Lentils Stew

Carrots Fennel Salad

Servings: 2

Ingredients:

- 1/3 cup lentils
- 2 cups vegetable stock or water
- ¼ red bell peppers, finely chopped
- 2 celery sticks, finely chopped
- 1 /4 white onion, finely chopped
- 1 clove garlic, grated

Spices: 2 stems of fresh thyme, 1 teaspoon sweet paprika, 1 bay leaves, 2 tablespoons finely chopped parsley, salt to taste

Instructions:

Rinse the lentils in a fine-mesh sieve and pick out any small stones or debris.

Combine the lentils, vegetables, thyme, bay leaves, sweet paprika and hot vegetable stock (or hot water) in a large saucepan over medium heat. Bring to a boil. Reduce the heat, simmer the lentils are tender, about 25 – 30 minutes. Remove from heat, add salt and parsley, and stir. Remove bay leaves; discard them. Serve in individual bowls.

Serve with: Carrots Fennel Salad

Ingredients: 2 medium carrots, ½ cup fennel, 1 stick celery, 1tablespoon olive oil, lemon juice to taste, 2 tablespoons finely chopped fresh parsley, a pinch of sea salt

Instructions: Wash the vegetables with cold water. Peel and cut into small, thin strips. Put them in a bowl. Add olive oil, lemon juice, parsley and salt, and mix

DINNER: Roasted Celeriac Root

Favourite Salad

Servings: 2

Ingredients:

- 1 medium celeriac root, peeled, cut into half-moon
- 2 tablespoons olive oil or sunflower oil

Spices: ground black pepper to taste, salt to taste

Instructions:

Preheat the oven to 390 F / 200 C.

Put the celeriac on a baking sheet. Sprinkle with pepper, salt and oil. Bake for 30 – 40 minutes until soft. Remove from oven, transfer celeriac in a bowl. Set aside.

Serve with: Favourite Salad

Ingredients: 4 torn fresh leaf lettuce, 3 cherry tomatoes cut into halves, 1 medium ripe avocado cut into small cubes, 3 finely chopped spring onions, 2 tablespoons finely chopped parsley, lemon juice to taste, sea salt to taste

Instructions: Prepare the salad just right before serving. In a large bowl, mix tomatoes, avocado, onion and leaf lettuce, parsley, salt to taste and lemon juice to taste. Stir the salad gently and serve.

DAY 11

LUNCH: Broccoli Brawn Basmati Rice

Peppers Tomato Salad

Servings: 2

Ingredients:

- 1 cup fresh broccoli flowers
- ½ cup brown basmati rice
- 2 tablespoons olive oil
- 1 minced clove garlic
- 1 teaspoon grated ginger
- ½ green chilli, finely chopped
- 1 yellow onion, finely chopped

Spices: 6 fresh mint leaves, 1 tablespoon finely chopped fresh coriander leaves, 1 tablespoon fresh lemon juice, salt to taste, 1 clove, a pinch of cinnamon, 1 cardamom.

Instructions:

Wash and soak rice in 1 1/3 cups of cold water. Then add fresh lemon juice and cook for 25 minutes. Once cooked, fluff it with a fork. Set aside.

Warm the oil over low heat in a large frying pan that has

a lid. Add cloves, cinnamon and cardamom, saute for 3 seconds. Add onions, green chilli; saute for 2 minutes and add garlic and ginger. Then add broccoli florets, salt to taste, mint and fresh coriander. Cover and cook for 3 minutes or until broccoli is fork-tender but still crunchy. Add the cooked rice and mix well.

Serve with: Peppers Tomato Salad

Ingredients: 3 baby sweet peppers - thinly sliced , 4 cherry tomatoes (halves), ¼ red onions (thinly) sliced, 1 tablespoon olive oil, salt to taste, 1 tablespoon finely chopped parsley

Instructions: Put the peppers, onions and tomatoes in a bowl, stir until thoroughly mixed. Before serving, season the vegetables with salt and oil, sprinkle with parsley.

DINNER: Roasted Chicken Breast Fillet

Fresh Kale Salad

Servings: 2

Ingredients:

- 11 oz (310 g), 2 chicken breast fillet, boneless & skinless
- 2 tablespoons vegetable oil

Spices: ¼ teaspoon smoked paprika, a pinch of ground black pepper, a pinch of thyme, a pinch of oregano, a pinch of rosemary, sea salt to taste.

Instructions:

Preheat the oven to 350 F (180 C).

Prepare a seasoning mixture. Put all the spices in a bowl and whisk until thoroughly mixed.

Drizzle the chicken breast with oil. Then rub with seasoning mixture.

Spray the baking tray with oil. Place chicken breast, roast until cooked through, 35 minutes. Remove from oven. Transfer the chicken breast to individual plates and allow to rest 5 – 6 minutes before serving.

Serve with: Fresh Kale Salad.

Ingredients: 7 oz (200 g) fresh leaf kale, sliced into small pieces; for the dressing: a tablespoon olive oil, 1 tablespoon lemon juice, 1 teaspoon apple cider vinegar, 1 teaspoon Worcestershire sauce, ½ tablespoon Dijon mustard, 1 minced clove garlic, a pinch of sea salt

Instructions: In a small bowl, whisk all ingredients for the dressing (you can use a blender).

Wash the kale well. Put it in a bowl. Pour the dressing and mix just right before serving.

DAY 12

LUNCH: Basted Eggs

Spicy Tomato Salad

Serving: 1

Ingredients:

- 3 large eggs
- 1-teaspoon butter

Spices: salt to taste, a pinch of sweet paprika, ground black pepper to taste.

Instructions:

Melted the butter in a non-stick skillet over medium heat. Add the eggs, being careful not to break the yolk. Cook until egg white is starting to set. Pour3 tablespoons of water and cover immediately. The steam will cook the top of the eggs. Cook for 1 – 2 minutes or until an opaque white film over the top of the egg yolk (depending on how well done you like your eggs.) Remove the skillet from the heat, remove the lid and serve immediately. Season with salt, sweet paprika and black pepper.

Serve with: Spicy Tomato Salad.

Ingredients: 5 chopped plum tomatoes, 1 finely chopped green chillies, 1 finely chopped spring onions, 1 teaspoon olive oil, 1 teaspoon lemon juice, a pinch sea salt, finely chopped fresh coriander to taste, 1 tablespoon finely chopped parsley, 6 olives

Instructions: In a large bowl, mix all ingredients and mix gently.

DINNER: Creamy Sweet Potato Soup

Garnish: Croutons

Serving: 2

Ingredients:

- 1 lb (450 g) sweet potato
- 1 small carrot
- 1small onion
- 2 sticks celery
- 2 tablespoons olive oil

Spices: 2 stems of fresh thyme, a pinch of ground black pepper, salt to taste, 2 tablespoons finely chopped fresh parsley, juice of ¼ lemon.

Instructions:

Peel the sweet potato and vegetables, rinse and cut into

rustic chunks.

Heat olive oil in a soup pot over medium-high heat. Add thyme, onion, carrots, sweet potato, celery and salt to taste, saute for 3 minutes. Pour 3 cups of hot water. Simmer for 30 minutes or until sweet potatoes are soft. Puree the mixture in a food processor or blender (or mash to desired consistency).

Before serving, stir in parsley and serve in individual bowls. Garnish with croutons.

Season with lemon juice, optional.

Serve with: Croutons

Ingredients: 3 medium slices wholemeal bread, 2 teaspoons olive oil, a pinch of sea salt, a pinch of ground black pepper

Instructions: Preheat the oven to 390 F / 200C. Cut bread into small cubes. Put the bread cubes on a baking sheet. Season with salt, ground black pepper and olive oil, mix until the bread is well coated. Bake it shaking the baking sheet occasionally until the cubes are lightly browned and crisp. Remove from the oven. Let cool.

DAY 13

LUNCH: Sautéed Potatoes with Spinach

Servings: 2

Ingredients:

- 12 oz (340 g) potatoes, cut into 1-inch (2.5 cm) pieces
- 7 oz (200 g) fresh leaf spinach, washed and ready to eat
- 1 medium carrot, cut into half moons
- ½ yellow onion, finely chopped
- ½ tablespoon fresh ginger, grated
- 1 clove garlic, grated
- 2 tablespoons olive oil

Spices: ½ teaspoon cumin seeds, salt to taste, ground black pepper to taste, 1 teaspoon crushed red pepper flakes, ½ tablespoon chopped cilantro, 2 tablespoons finely chopped parsley.

Instructions:

Heat oil in a skillet over medium-high heat. Add in the cumin seeds for a few seconds until they sizzle. Add onion and ginger and cook for 2 minutes or until softened. Add carrots, potatoes, ground black pepper, salt, and ½-cup hot water. Cover with a lid, reduce heat and simmer for 15 minutes until potatoes are tender to the touch. Then add spinach leaves and stir well. Cook for 3 minutes, stirring occasionally. If there is any excess liquid accumulated, increase heat to evaporate it. Stir in crushed red pepper flakes, chopped fresh leaves of coriander and parsley. Transfer to serving plates.

DINNER: Fish Patties

Cucumber Fennel Salad

Servings: 2

Ingredients:

- 10 oz (280 g) fresh skinless & boneless salmon fillet

Spices: grated zest of 1 lime, 1 tablespoon lime juice, 1 tablespoon finely chopped leaf parsley, 2 stems of fresh thyme, ground black pepper to taste, salt to taste

Instructions:

Chop the salmon fillet into pieces. Place them in a food processor or food chopper, pulse for about 3 seconds (be careful not to make a mess). Place the fish in a large bowl. Combine with all spices. Divide into four and shape into 4 patties.

Preheat grill (or grill pan) to medium heat. Use Non-flammable cooking spray to grease the grill.

Grill fish patties until a crust on both sides (about 5 minutes on each side).

Serve with: Cucumber Fennel Salad.

Ingredients: ½ cucumber (cut into thin strips), ½ fresh fennel loose, ½ cup celery fresh and crunchy (cut into thin strips), 1 tablespoon fresh finely chopped dill, sea salt to taste;

For the dressing: 2 tablespoons olive oil, 1 tablespoon lime juice, 1 teaspoon mustard

Instructions: In a small bowl, make the dressing. In a large bowl, combine vegetables, spices and dressing.

Serve the fish patties with the fresh fennel salad.

DAY14

LUNCH: Turkey Breast with Thyme Rosemary

Servings: 2

Ingredients:

- 9oz (250 g) turkey diced breast
- 1 onion, chopped
- 1/3 red bell peppers, chopped
- 2 sticks celery, finely chopped
- 1 small parsnip, cut into thin half-moons
- 1clove garlic, grated
- 2 tablespoons olive oil

Spices: 2 stems of fresh thyme, 1 small sprig of fresh rosemary, 1 teaspoon sweet paprika, 1 teaspoon Worcestershire sauce, 1 tablespoon finely chopped leaf parsley, ground black pepper to taste, salt to taste, crushed chilli flakes to taste (optional).

Instructions:

Season turkey breast with salt and ground black pepper. Heat the oil in a large non – stick frying pan over medium heat. Add the turkey, and cook on all sides for 2 minutes, stirring occasionally.

Then add the onion, garlic, parsnip, red bell peppers, celery, fresh thyme and sprig fresh rosemary, saute 2 minutes, stirring occasionally. Add Worcestershire sauce, sweet paprika, salt, pepper, crushed chilli flakes to taste (optional) and 2/3 cup hot water. Cover, and reduce heat to low, simmer for 40 minutes or until the turkey tender.

Serve the dish on individual plates, sprinkle with finely chopped parsley.

DINNER: Onion Soup

Garnish: Seeded Baguette

Servings: 2

Ingredients:

- 2 white onions
- 1 tablespoon flour
- 2 teaspoons butter
- 2 ½ cups vegetable broth

Spices: crushed chilli flakes, 2 stems of fresh thyme, ground black pepper and salt to taste.

Instructions:

Peel, wash and cut the onion into thin slices. In a

saucepan, melt butter over medium heat. Add the thyme and onions to stew, stirring occasionally. When acquiring a brownish colour, add crushed chilli flakes and flour. Stir and add trickle cold broth, ground black pepper and salt to taste. Simmer the soup for 10 minutes. Remove the saucepan from heat.

Serve with: Seeded Baguette

Ingredients: ¼ seeded baguette, 1 clove garlic, 1-tablespoon olive oil, a pinch crushed dried basil or oregano.

Instructions: Cut the baguette into slices. Rub them with a clove of garlic. Mix in a bowl the olive oil and basil. Apply a light coating on the slices with this mixture. Bake them in the oven at 392 F / 200 C, until golden brown. Remove from oven. Set aside to cool.

Place at the bottom of individual bowls for soup 2 slices baguette. Pour over hot soup and serve.

DAY15

LUNCH: Peas with Mint

Beetroot and Celeriac Salad

Servings: 2

Ingredients:

- 6 oz (170 g) fresh or frozen peas shelled
- 6 white pearl onions (small white onions), whole
- ½ yellow onions, cut into cubes
- 1 large carrot, cut into half-moons
- 3 lettuce leaves, torn
- 2 tablespoon olive oil

Spices: 6 leaves of fresh mint (torn), a bay leaf, ground black pepper to taste, sea salt to taste

Instructions:

Heat in saucepan olive oil over medium-high heat. Add and sauté the yellow onions, white pearl onions and carrots for 3 minutes. Then add peas, salt, ground black pepper and enough water to cover barely. Cook over high heat for 2 minutes, add bay leaf. Continue until the peas are tender, a few more minutes. Then add torn mint leaves and lettuce leaves, stir and remove from heat.

Serve with: Beetroot and Celeriac Salad

Ingredients: 1 cup peeled and shredded beetroot, ½ cup peeled and shredded celeriac; 2 tablespoons lemon juice, 1 - 2 tablespoons olive oil, salt to taste, 2 sprigs of fresh dill and 4 lemon wedges for garnish

Instructions: Prepare the salad just right before serving. In a bowl, mix beetroot, celeriac, lemon juice, olive oil and salt to taste. Serve in individual plates, garnish with fresh dill and lemon wedges.

DINNER: Roasted Pork Rib Rack

Garnish: Roasted Vegetables

Servings: 2

Ingredients:

- 18 oz (500 g) fresh pork loin rib rack
- 1 yellow onion, cut into halves
- 1 red bell pepper, cut into quarters lengthwise
- 2 medium carrots, sliced thinly lengthwise

For the marinade: 1 clove garlic - crushed, 1 teaspoon smoked paprika, 1 teaspoon tomato paste, 1 tablespoon oil, ground black pepper to taste, a pinch of nutmeg, 1 pinch of cumin powder, oregano to taste

Instructions:

Prepare the marinade. In a large bowl, combine all ingredients, and mix well. Rub the pork ribs on both sides with marinade. Cover with plastic food wrap and place in the fridge for 4 hours or overnight. Do not forget to upturn them from time to time.

Preheat the oven to 350 F (180 C).

Carefully grease the baking tray with oil. Place pork ribs, ¼-cup hot water and cover paper aluminium. Roast 60 minutes, remove paper aluminium and add onion, carrots and peppers. Increase the temperature to 390 F / 200 C and roast 15 minutes or until a crust.

Transfer the pork ribs and vegetables to individual plates and allow to rest 5 minutes before serving.

DAY16

LUNCH: Cheese & Garlic Stuffed Mushrooms

Avocado Tomatoes Salad

Servings: 2

Ingredients:

- 9 oz (250 g), 2 large Portabello mushrooms
- 2 oz (50 g) grated four-cheese mix
- 2 cloves garlic, minced
- ¼ medium onion, finely chopped
- 1 tablespoon olive oil

Spices: 1 teaspoon fresh thyme, 1 tablespoon finely chopped parsley, ½ tablespoon finely chopped dill, salt to taste, ground black pepper to taste.

Instructions:

Using a kitchen towel, brush the mushrooms. Remove the stems of the mushrooms and cut them into small pieces. Heat oil in a saucepan over medium heat. Add the onions and chopped mushrooms stems, saute for about 2 minutes, occasionally stirring. Add the garlic, thyme and parsley, and then cook 30 seconds, stirring. Remove from heat. Set aside, mixture to cool.

Preheat the oven to 390 F / 200 C.

Stir the cheeses into the cooled mixture and stuff the mushrooms caps. Arrange them to a rimmed baking sheet. Bake the mushrooms until the cheese has melted and mushrooms have softened – for about 15 minutes. Remove from the oven and transfer the stuffed mushrooms to individual plates. Sprinkle ground black pepper to taste and fresh dill. Serve immediately with salad.

Serve with Avocado Tomatoes Salad.

Ingredients: 1 medium ripe & ready avocado (peeled, pitted and cubed), 3 cherry tomatoes (quarters), 1/3 yellow bell peppers (thinly strips sliced), 1 tablespoon fresh finely chopped coriander, 1 clove garlic (minced), 1 tablespoon lemon juice, sea salt to taste; for serving:4 fresh leaves lettuce and 2 lemon wedges

Instructions: Prepare the salad just right before serving. Put all ingredients in a bowl and mix gently. Put to an individual serving plate 2 lettuce leaves, on them ½ of the salad, sprinkle with coriander and add 2 lemon wedges.

DINNER: Roasted Potato and Cauliflower

Iceberg and Sunflower Seeds Salad

Servings: 2

Ingredients:

- 12 oz (340 g) baby potatoes
- 14 oz (400 g) cauliflower florets
- 3 cloves garlic, chopped
- 3 tablespoons sunflower oil

Spices: 1-teaspoon garam masala, ground black pepper to taste, sea salt to taste, 2 finely chopped spring onions.

Instructions:

Preheat the oven to 390 F / 200 C. Spray a baking tray with cooking spray (or grease with oil). Set aside.

Mix potatoes, cauliflower florets, garlic, garam masala, ground black pepper, and salt to taste in a large bowl. Stir and spread the mixture on a baking tray. Drizzle over oil and roast until nicely browned, about 35 minutes, stirring once halfway through. Sprinkle with spring onions and serve.

Serve with: Iceberg with Sunflower Seeds Salad.

Ingredients: ½ Iceberg lettuce - torn into small pieces, 2 finely chopped spring onions, 1 teaspoon apple cider vinegar, 6 green olives, 1 tablespoon sunflower oil, sea salt to taste; garnish: 1 tablespoon raw sunflower seeds

Instructions: Put all ingredients in a bowl and mix gently. Sprinkle with sunflower seeds and serve.

DAY 17

LUNCH: Curry Brawn Rice

Servings: 2

Ingredients:

- ½ cup brown basmati rice
- 1 small Granny Smith apple, finely chopped
- ½ yellow onion, finely chopped
- 2 tablespoons sunflower oil
- 1.5 cup hot vegetable broth

Spices: 1-teaspoon curry powder, ground black pepper to taste, sea salt to taste, 2 Granny Smith apple wedges.

Instructions:

In a medium skillet, over medium-high heat, heat sunflower oil. Add onion and finely chopped apple, saute for 2 minutes. Add the rice and cook a minute, stirring continuously. Add curry powder and hot vegetable broth and stir. Bring to a boil. Simmer until the rice absorbs the liquid. Remove from heat. Garnish with apple wedges and serve.

DINNER: Chicken Broccoli Soup

Servings: 2

Ingredients:

- 8 oz (225 g) fresh chicken breast, boneless & skinless
- ¼ white onions, finely chopped
- ¼ cup celeriac, finely chopped
- 1 small parsnip, finely chopped
- 1 teaspoon grated ginger
- 3.5 oz (100 g) fresh broccoli florets
- 2 cups chicken broth, low sodium or water
- 1 teaspoon butter

Spices: 1-teaspoon fresh thyme, 1 bay leave, ground black pepper to taste, sea salt to taste, 1 tablespoon finely chopped parsley, lemon juice to taste (optional).

Instructions:

Rinse, dry and cut the chicken breast into small pieces.

Heat the butter in a soup pot over medium heat. Add the chicken and cook, about 2 minutes until white, stirring continuously. Add the onion, ginger, celeriac, parsnip, bay leaves, fresh thyme, black pepper, and salt to taste; cook for 2 minutes, stirring occasionally. Add the chicken broth. Bring to boil. Reduce heat to low and simmer until the chicken is tender.

Then remove the lid, add broccoli florets and cook for 4 minutes. Remove from heat. Serve the soup in individual bowls. Sprinkle parsley and season with lemon juice to taste (optional).

Serve with Lettuce Sunflower Seeds Salad

Ingredients: 4 handfuls leaf lettuces, 2 finely chopped spring onions, 3.5 oz (100 g) grated Mozzarella cheese, 0.5 oz (15 g) raw peeled sunflower seeds; for the dressing: 1tablespoon olive oil, 2 tablespoons fresh lemon juice, ½ teaspoon mustard, salt to taste, ground black pepper to taste.

Instructions: In a small bowl, mix all ingredients for the dressing and stir.

Wash, dry with a kitchen towel, and shred into small pieces the lettuce. Put in a large bowl. Add onions and sunflower seeds and mix. Drizzle over the dressing and mix just right before serving. Serve in individual bowls and sprinkle with grated Mozzarella cheese.

DAY 18

LUNCH: Pinto Bean Stuffed Peppers

Green Salad

Servings: 2

Ingredients:

- 2 red (or green) bell peppers
- 1 cup (canned) pinto beans, rinsed, drained
- 1/4 yellow onion
- 1 clove garlic, minced
- 2 tablespoons sunflower oil

Spices: ½ teaspoon Cajun seasoning, sea salt to taste, 1 tablespoon finely chopped parsley for garnish.

Instructions:

Preheat oven to 390 F / 200 C.

Heat 1-tablespoon oil in a small skillet over medium heat. Saute onion in the oil for 1 – 2 minutes, occasionally stirring, until it is soft. Stir in bean, garlic and Cajun seasoning, cook until hot. Remove from heat. Set aside.

Cut a thin slice from the stem end of each bell pepper to remove the top of the pepper. Remove seeds and membranes. Rinse peppers and season with salt. Stuff them with bean mixture. Grease a small baking dish, place peppers, and pour 1-tablespoon oil over them. Cover tightly with aluminium foil. Bake 15 minutes. Uncover and bake another 15 minutes until peppers are tender. Sprinkle with parsley and serve.

Serve with: Green Salad

Ingredients: ½ Iceberg Lettuce, a handful of fresh arugula, 1 small ripe avocado (cut into cubes), ½ English cucumber (cut into tiny disks), 2 finely chopped spring onions, 1 tablespoon sunflower oil, salt to taste, apple cider vinegar to taste (optional), 2 tablespoons finely chopped parsley

Instructions: Put all ingredients in a large bowl and mix gently. Sprinkle with parsley and serve.

DINNER: Vegetarian Pizza with Homemade Dough

Servings: 2

Ingredients:

For the dough: 1 cup wholemeal flour, 1 teaspoon active dry yeast, a pinch of sugar, a pinch of sea salt, about ½ cup warm water, 1 tablespoon olive oil, 2 tablespoons cornmeal

Topping:
- 2 tablespoons olive oil
- ½ cup raw minced tomatoes
- 1 small red onion, cut into thin disks
- ½ red bell peppers, cut into thin strips
- 2 tablespoons green olives, sliced
- 3.5 oz (100 g) mushrooms, sliced
- 1 tablespoon cornmeal
- 1 teaspoon oregano, salt and ground black pepper to taste, 8 leaves fresh basil

Instructions:

First, prepare the dough:

In a large bowl, dissolve yeast in warm water. Add the sugar, olive oil, salt and a tablespoon of flour, whisk until smooth. Stir in enough remaining flour to form a stiff dough. Transfer it onto a floured surface. Knead the dough 3 minutes. The dough must be smooth and elastic. Place in a greased bowl, turning once to grease the top. Cover with plastic wrap and leave to rise 45 minutes (in a warm).

Preheat the oven to 390 F / 200 C. In a large bowl, put red onion, bell peppers and mushrooms, season with salt and ground black pepper to taste.

Grease a large pizza pan and sprinkle it with cornmeal. Roll the dough out with a thickness of 0.2 inches (0.5 cm). Transfer it to the pizza pan. Pinch edges to form a rim. Cover and let rest 15 minutes. Then bake 8 minutes or until edges are lightly browned. Remove from oven. Spread 3 tablespoons of minced tomatoes over the top of the dough (leaving around a border of 1 inch / 2.5 cm at the edges). Sprinkle with oregano. Then add the vegetables, mushrooms and olives, drizzle with a tablespoon of olive oil.

Increase the heat to 450 F / 230 C. Bake for 8 minutes until the crust is golden brown. Remove from the oven, and cut the pizza into pieces. Add the remaining minced tomatoes and basil; serve immediately.

DAY 19

LUNCH: Vegan Asparagus Quinoa

Servings: 2

- Ingredients:
- 1/3 cup quinoa
- 6 asparagus, peeled
- 6 cherry tomatoes, halved
- 2 spring onions, finely chopped
- 2 tablespoons roasted chopped hazelnuts
- 1 cup vegetable stock
- 2 tablespoons of olive oil

Spices: a pinch of ground black pepper, salt to taste, ½ lemon juice, 6 fresh leaves basil, 2 lemon wedges.

Instructions:

Pour the quinoa with 2 cups of cold water and leave for 2 hours. Then rinse thoroughly with cold water. Heat vegetable stock in a saucepan over low heat. Add the quinoa, put the lid and cook for 10 minutes. Remove from the heat. Set it aside until it absorbs the liquid- for about 5 minutes. Then add tomatoes, onions, a pinch of black pepper, salt to taste, basil and olive oil, stir gently. Serve in individual plates.

Pour a cup of water into a saucepan. Bring to a boil. Add a pinch of salt and the asparagus. Cook 2 minutes, remove from heat and drain. Serve the asparagus over the quinoa mixture. Sprinkle with ground black pepper and roasted chopped hazelnuts. Garnish with lemon wedges.

DINNER: Beef Burgers

Garnish: Guacamole

Servings: 2

Ingredients:

- 12 oz (340 g) beef mince, 20% fat
- 1 teaspoon tomatoes paste

Spices: 1-teaspoon Worcestershire sauce, 1 tablespoon finely chopped parsley, 1 teaspoon fresh thyme, ½-teaspoon sweet paprika, ground black pepper to taste, salt to taste.

Instructions:

In a medium bowl, put beef mince, tomatoes paste, and all spices, mix gently. Shape the mixture into 2 burgers.

Preheat grill (or grill pan) to medium heat. Use Non-flammable cooking spray to grease the grill. Bake burgers until lightly browned on both sides (about 5 minutes on each side).

Serve with lettuce leaf and guacamole.

Serve with: Guacamole

Ingredients: a large ripe & ready avocado, 1/3 cup fresh tomatoes cut into small cubes, 1 finely chopped spring onion, 5 torn fresh basil leaves, 1-tablespoon lime juice, salt to taste

Instructions: In a small bowl, mash avocado with a fork. Add lime juice, tomatoes, basil, and onions. Season with salt. Mix gently.

DAY 20

LUNCH: Lettuce Salad Hard Boiled Eggs

Aioli Sauce

Servings: 2

Ingredients:

- 4 handfuls fresh leaf lettuce, torn
- 2 large free-range eggs, hard-boiled, cut into quarters
- 2 spring onions, finely chopped
- 8 cherry tomatoes, halved

Instructions:

Put leaf lettuce, spring onions and tomatoes in a large bowl, mix gently. Arrange eggs on top. Serve immediately, garnished aioli sauce

Serve with: Aioli Sauce

Ingredients: 1 egg, 1 egg yolk, 2 crushed clove garlic, 1 tablespoon lemon juice, 1 tablespoon Dijon mustard, ½ teaspoon of sea salt, 1 cup olive oil or sunflower oil

Instructions: Blend egg, egg yolk, garlic, lemon juice,

Dijon mustard, sea salt in a blender. Process it at high speed for 2 minutes. Then while the blender is running, pour the olive oil (or sunflower oil) in parts. In about 2 minutes, open the machine. Aioli sauce is ready. Use 2 tablespoons for each serving.

Note: The remaining amount of Aioli sauce can keep well in the refrigerator, covered for several days.

DINNER: Baked Carrot Patties and Sauce

Herbs Tomato Italian Salad

Servings: 2

Ingredients:

- 12 oz (340 g) carrots, peel, grated
- 3.5 oz (100 g) parsnips, peel, grated
- 1 clove garlic, grated
- 1 teaspoon ginger, shredded
- 3 tablespoons wholemeal flour or breadcrumbs
- 3 tablespoons sunflower oil

Spices: a pinch of nutmeg, ½-teaspoon turmeric powder, a pinch of ground black pepper, salt to taste

Instructions:

Preheat oven to 360 F (180 C). Prepared baking tray lined with parchment paper.

Warm 1 tablespoon of the oil over medium heat in a large frying pan that has a lid. Add garlic, ginger, parsnips, and carrots, stir. Cover and cook for 2 – 3 minutes until the vegetables are fork-tender but still crunchy. Remove from heat. Transfer the mixture to a large bowl to cool. Add all spices, wholemeal flour or breadcrumbs and 2 tablespoons oil, mix until well combined.

Shape patties (the number depends on their size). Place them on a baking tray. Bake for 25 minutes; after 15 minutes, flip the patties (use tongs) until the patties are firm and baked through.

Garnish to taste: Almond Sauce

Ingredients: 2 oz (55 g) ground almonds, 1 minced clove garlic, 2 Roma tomatoes, 1 teaspoon sweet paprika, 6 fresh basil leaves, 3 tablespoons olive oil, 1 tablespoon apple cider vinegar

Instructions: Dip the tomatoes for 1 minute in boiling water. Remove them and peel. Beat with a mixer the garlic, tomatoes and almonds. Add the paprika, basil and vinegar. To this mixture, add the oil in a thin stream, stirring vigorously.

<u>Serve with</u> Herbs Tomato Italian Salad

Ingredients: 2 medium slices wholemeal bread, 1 teaspoon butter, 8 cherry tomatoes (halved), 2 minced clove garlic, ½ finely chopped red onion, 1 tablespoon olive oil, lemon juice to taste, 1 handful of mixed fresh herbs (finely chopped basil, rosemary, parsley, thyme, tarragon) a pinch of sea salt, a pinch of ground black pepper

Instructions: Preheat the oven to 390 F / 200C. Cut bread into small cubes. In a small skillet, melt the butter over low heat. Put the bread, stir and after 2 minutes, transfer in a baking sheet. Bake until browned. Remove from the oven. Let the croutons cool.

In a large bowl, mix all vegetables, herbs, spices, oil, and lemon juice. Stir gently and serve in individual plates. Add on top croutons.

DAY 21

LUNCH: Minestrone Soup

Garnish: Basil Pesto

Servings: 2

Ingredients:

- ¼ medium yellow onions, chopped
- 1 minced clove garlic
- 1 medium potato, cut into small cubes
- 1 small carrot, finely chopped
- ½ small zucchini, chopped
- 1 handful green beans, halved
- 1/3 cup tomatoes, diced
- 1 handful macaroni
- 2 tablespoon olive oil

Spices: 2 stems of fresh thyme, sea salt to taste, ground black pepper to taste.

Instructions:

Heat the olive oil in a soup pot over medium heat. Add the onion and garlic and saute 2 minutes. Stir in the potatoes, carrots, zucchini, thyme, salt, and saute for 2 – 3 minutes. Add the green beans and 3 cups hot water and simmer for 15 minutes. Add the macaroni and tomatoes, cook 8 – 9 minutes. Remove from heat. Serve the soup in individual bowls with garnish.

Serve with: Basil Pesto.

Ingredients: 4 handfuls fresh basil, 2 cloves crushed garlic, 2 tablespoons pine nuts, 1/3 cup olive oil, salt to taste

Instructions: Bake the pine nuts in a dry pan for a few minutes. Cut them into small pieces. Wash the basil leaves and dry them well. Cut them into very small pieces. Add the crushed garlic and pine nuts. Put all the products in a blender for 2 - 3 seconds. Transfer the mixture into a bowl. Add a trickle of olive oil. Stir the mixture carefully. Garnish the soup with 1-teaspoon basil pesto.

Pour the remaining pesto into a glass jar and close it with a cap. Keep it in a cool place.

DINNER: White Fish Skewers

Chimichurri Sauce

Servings: 2

Ingredients:

- 12 oz (340 g) fresh white fish fillet, boneless & skinless
- 1 yellow onion
- ½ green bell peppers
- ½ red bell peppers
- A pinch of sea salt, a pinch of ground black

Instructions:

Cut the fish on cubes of equal size (1 - 1.2 inch/ 2.5 - 3 cm). Rub with salt and pepper.

Cut the onion and peppers into pieces for skewers.

Preheat grill to medium heat. Add a small amount of vegetable oil on a folded piece of paper towel, and then carefully grease the grill with the oil.

Thread 3 - 4 pieces of fish, 1 piece of onion, 1 piece of red pepper, 1 piece of green pepper to each skewer. Cook on the grill for 6 minutes, turning regularly, or until the fish and vegetables are cooked through.

Serve fish skewers warm with sauce.

Serve with: Chimichurri Sauce

Ingredients: ½ cup olive oil or vegetable oil, 2 tablespoons red wine vinegar, 4 tablespoons finely chopped parsley, 3 minced cloves garlic, 1 tablespoon finely chopped chilli, pinch dried oregano, 4 tablespoons finely chopped parsley, sea salt to taste, ground black pepper to taste

Instructions: In a medium bowl, mix all ingredients. Stir well; use the sauce after 10 minutes. Chimichurri sauce can be prepared, cover, and refrigerated before serving.

*Note: **The remaining amount of Chimichurri sauce can keep well in the refrigerator, covered for several days.***

R . L a z a r o v a

FOR YOUR NOTES:

Healthy weight loss

Printed in Great Britain
by Amazon

24855588R00056